# 50 Amazing U.S. Mazes

## Journey Through The USA!

### by Dan Nevins

Miss Rita

Watermill Press

# Ready for fun?

In this exciting book, you'll find a maze for each of the 50 U.S. states! So sit back, pick up a pencil, and get ready for an incredible journey of twists and turns. If you get stuck, answers begin on page 53.

# ALABAMA

Done

**Capital:** Montgomery
**Nickname:** Heart of Dixie
**State Bird:** yellowhammer
**State Flower:** camellia

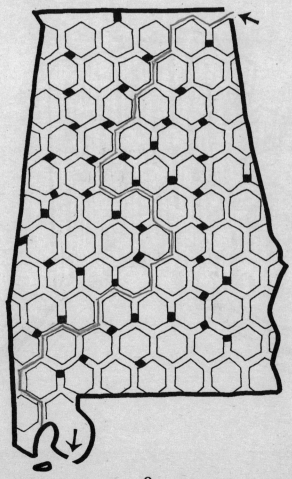

# ALASKA

Done

**Capital:** Juneau
**Nickname:** Last Frontier
**State Bird:** willow ptarmigan
**State Flower:** forget-me-not

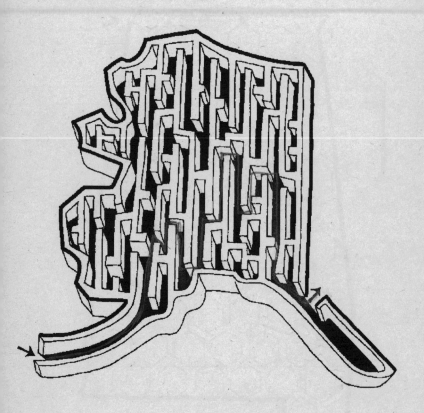

# ARIZONA

**Capital:** Phoenix
**Nickname:** Grand Canyon State
**State Bird:** cactus wren
**State Flower:** saguaro cactus flower

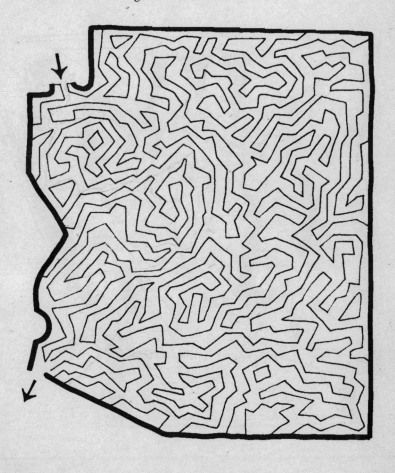

# ARKANSAS

**Capital:** Little Rock
**Nickname:** Land of Opportunity
**State Bird:** mockingbird
**State Flower:** apple blossom

# CALIFORNIA

*Done*

**Capital:** Sacramento
**Nickname:** Golden State
**State Bird:** California valley quail
**State Flower:** golden poppy

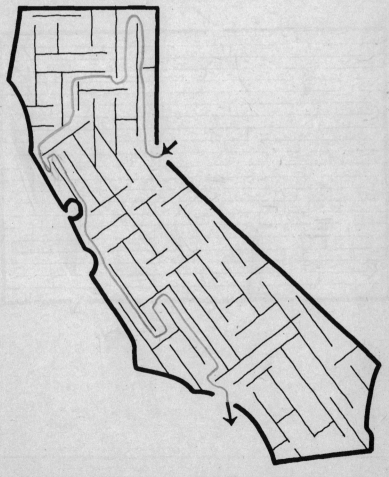

# COLORADO

*Done*

**Capital:** Denver
**Nickname:** Centennial State
**State Bird:** lark bunting
**State Flower:** Rocky Mountain columbine

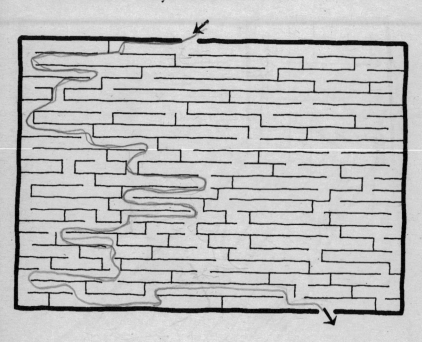

# CONNECTICUT

**Capital:** Hartford
**Nickname:** Constitution State
**State Bird:** robin
**State Flower:** mountain laurel

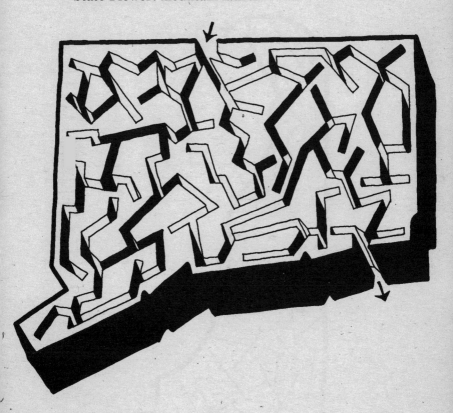

# DELAWARE

*Done*

**Capital:** Dover
**Nickname:** First State
**State Bird:** blue hen chicken
**State Flower:** peach blossom

# FLORIDA

Done

**Capital:** Tallahassee
**Nickname:** Sunshine State
**State Bird:** mockingbird
**State Flower:** orange blossom

# GEORGIA

**Capital:** Atlanta
**Nickname:** Empire State of the South
**State Bird:** brown thrasher
**State Flower:** Cherokee rose

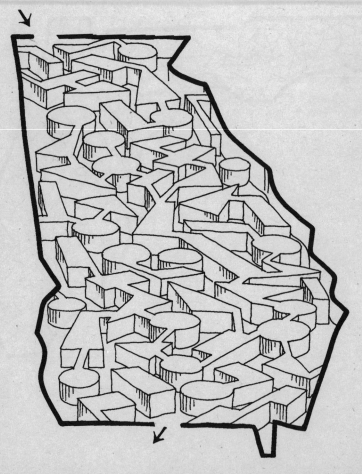

# HAWAII

Done

**Capital:** Honolulu
**Nickname:** Aloha State
**State Bird:** Hawaiian goose
**State Flower:** yellow hibiscus

# IDAHO

**Capital:** Boise
**Nickname:** Gem State
**State Bird:** mountain bluebird
**State Flower:** syringa

14

# ILLINOIS

*Done*

**Capital:** Springfield
**Nickname:** Land of Lincoln
**State Bird:** cardinal
**State Flower:** violet

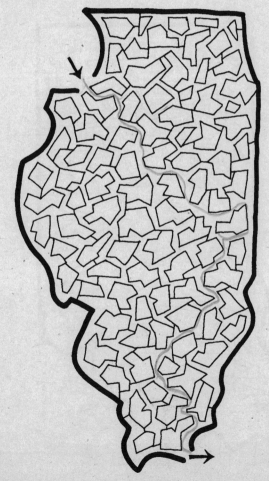

# INDIANA

**Capital:** Indianapolis
**Nickname:** Hoosier State
**State Bird:** cardinal
**State Flower:** peony

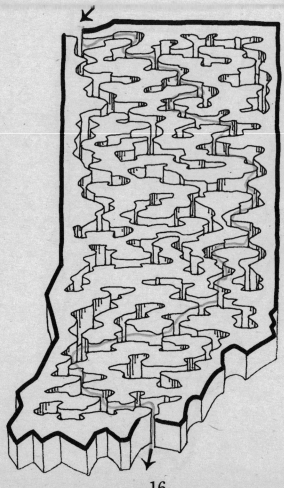

16

# IOWA

**Capital:** Des Moines
**Nickname:** Hawkeye State
**State Bird:** eastern goldfinch
**State Flower:** wild rose

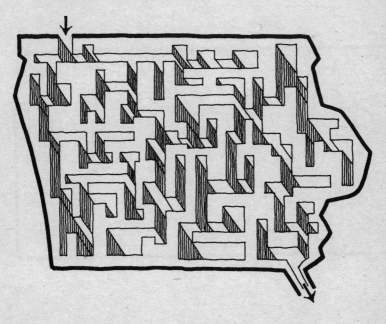

# KANSAS

*Done*

**Capital:** Topeka
**Nickname:** Sunflower State
**State Bird:** western meadowlark
**State Flower:** sunflower

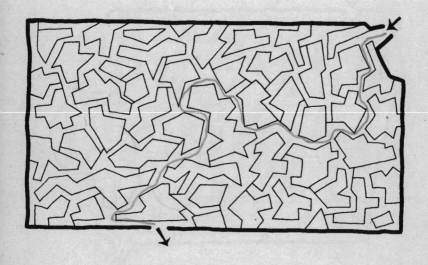

# KENTUCKY

**Capital:** Frankfort
**Nickname:** Bluegrass State
**State Bird:** cardinal
**State Flower:** goldenrod

# LOUISIANA

Done

**Capital:** Baton Rouge
**Nickname:** Pelican State
**State Bird:** brown pelican
**State Flower:** magnolia

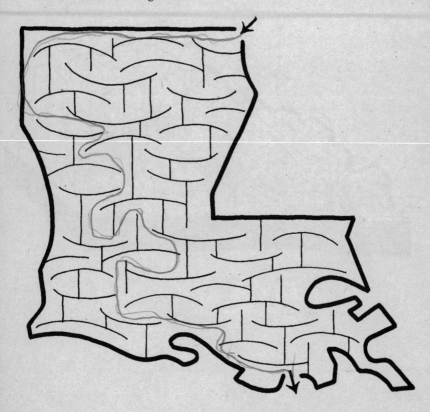

# MAINE

**Capital:** Augusta
**Nickname:** Pine Tree State
**State Bird:** chickadee
**State Flower:** white pine cone and tassel

21

# MARYLAND

Done

**Capital:** Annapolis
**Nickname:** Old Line State
**State Bird:** Baltimore oriole
**State Flower:** black-eyed Susan

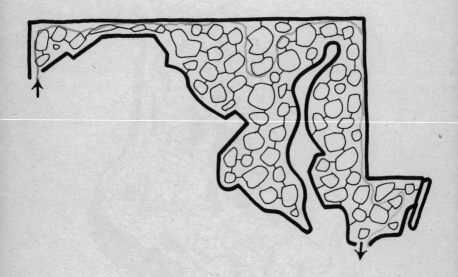

# MASSACHUSETTS Done

**Capital:** Boston
**Nickname:** Bay State
**State Bird:** chickadee
**State Flower:** mayflower

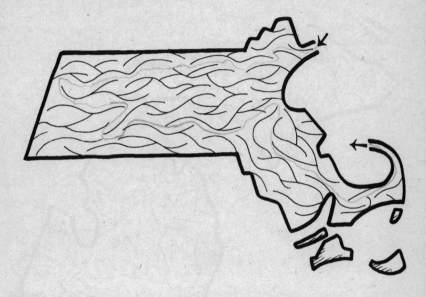

# MICHIGAN

Done

**Capital:** Lansing
**Nickname:** Wolverine State
**State Bird:** robin
**State Flower:** apple blossom

# MINNESOTA

Done

**Capital:** St. Paul
**Nickname:** Gopher State
**State Bird:** common loon
**State Flower:** pink and white lady's-slipper

25

# MISSISSIPPI

*Done*

**Capital:** Jackson
**Nickname:** Magnolia State
**State Bird:** mockingbird
**State Flower:** magnolia

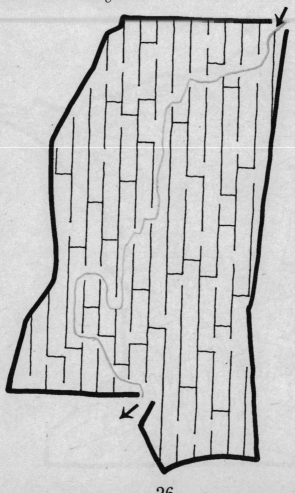

# MISSOURI

*Done*

**Capital:** Jefferson City
**Nickname:** Show Me State
**State Bird:** bluebird
**State Flower:** hawthorn

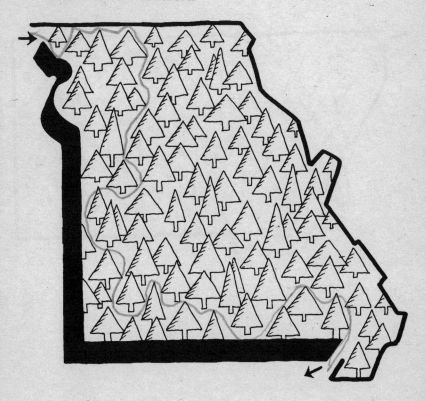

# MONTANA

_Done_

**Capital:** Helena
**Nickname:** Treasure State
**State Bird:** western meadowlark
**State Flower:** bitterroot

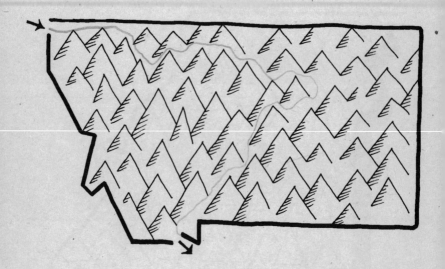

# NEBRASKA

**Capital:** Lincoln
**Nickname:** Cornhusker State
**State Bird:** western meadowlark
**State Flower:** goldenrod

# NEVADA

**Capital:** Carson City
**Nickname:** Silver State
**State Bird:** mountain bluebird
**State Flower:** sagebrush

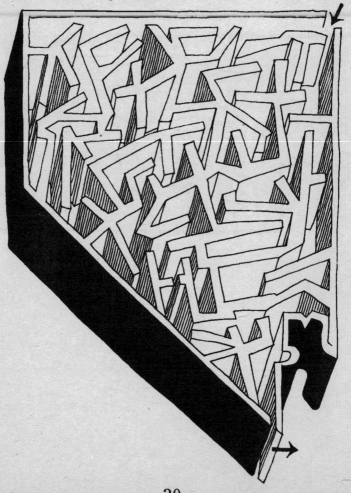

# NEW HAMPSHIRE

*Done*

**Capital:** Concord
**Nickname:** Granite State
**State Bird:** purple finch
**State Flower:** purple lilac

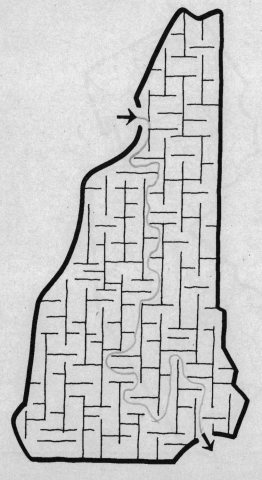

# NEW JERSEY

*Done*

**Capital:** Trenton
**Nickname:** Garden State
**State Bird:** eastern goldfinch
**State Flower:** purple violet

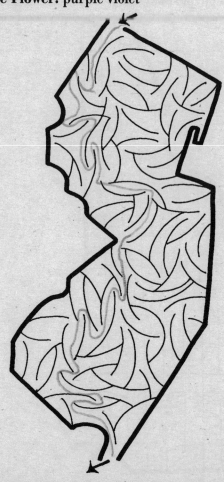

# NEW MEXICO

*Done*

**Capital:** Santa Fe
**Nickname:** Land of Enchantment
**State Bird:** roadrunner
**State Flower:** yucca

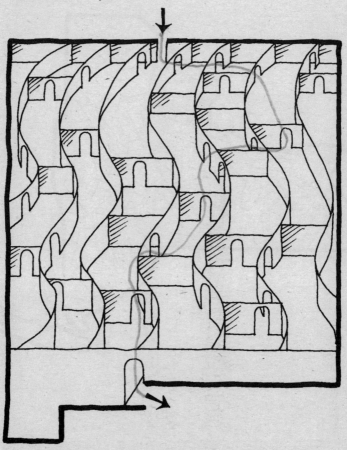

# NEW YORK

Done

**Capital:** Albany
**Nickname:** Empire State
**State Bird:** bluebird
**State Flower:** rose

# NORTH CAROLINA

**Capital:** Raleigh
**Nickname:** Tar Heel State
**State Bird:** cardinal
**State Flower:** flowering dogwood

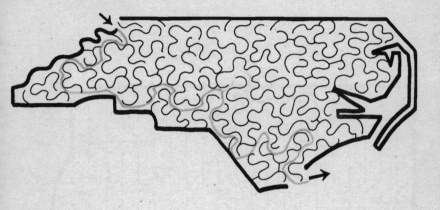

# NORTH DAKOTA

*Done*

**Capital:** Bismarck
**Nickname:** Flickertail State
**State Bird:** western meadowlark
**State Flower:** wild prairie rose

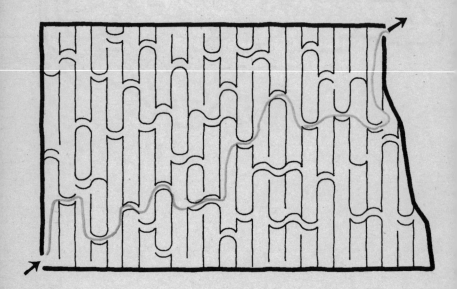

# OHIO

*Done*

**Capital:** Columbus
**Nickname:** Buckeye State
**State Bird:** cardinal
**State Flower:** scarlet carnation

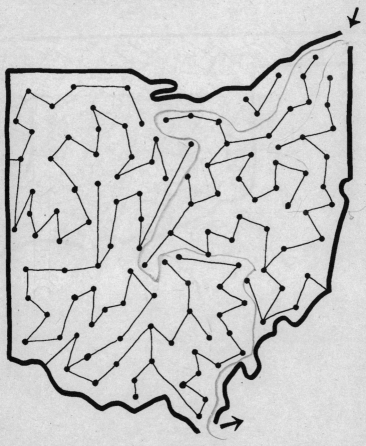

# OKLAHOMA

*Done*

**Capital:** Oklahoma City
**Nickname:** Sooner State
**State Bird:** scissor-tailed flycatcher
**State Flower:** mistletoe

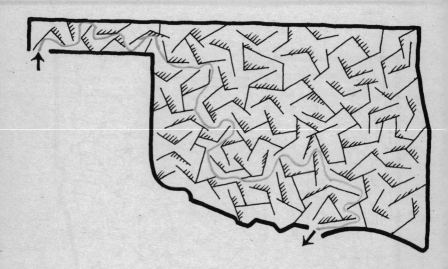

# OREGON

**Capital:** Salem
**Nickname:** Beaver State
**State Bird:** western meadowlark
**State Flower:** Oregon grape

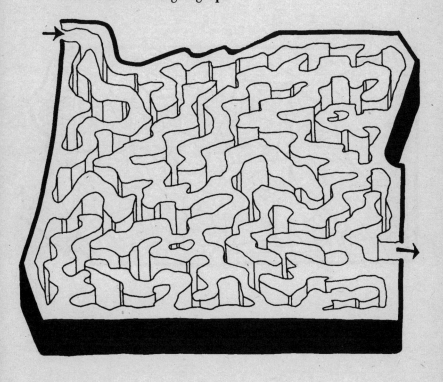

# PENNSYLVANIA

Done

**Capital:** Harrisburg
**Nickname:** Keystone State
**State Bird:** ruffed grouse
**State Flower:** mountain laurel

# RHODE ISLAND

Done

**Capital:** Providence
**Nickname:** Ocean State
**State Bird:** Rhode Island Red
**State Flower:** violet

# SOUTH CAROLINA

Done

**Capital:** Columbia
**Nickname:** Palmetto State
**State Bird:** Carolina wren
**State Flower:** Carolina jessamine

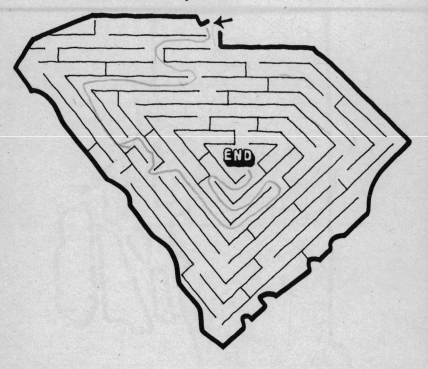

# SOUTH DAKOTA Done

**Capital:** Pierre
**Nickname:** Sunshine State
**State Bird:** ring-necked pheasant
**State Flower:** American pasqueflower

# TENNESSEE

*Done*

**Capital:** Nashville
**Nickname:** Volunteer State
**State Bird:** mockingbird
**State Flower:** iris

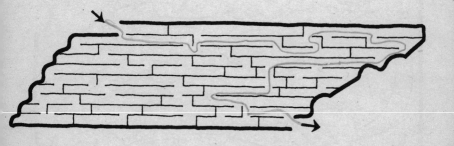

# TEXAS

Done.

**Capital:** Austin
**Nickname:** Lone Star State
**State Bird:** mockingbird
**State Flower:** bluebonnet

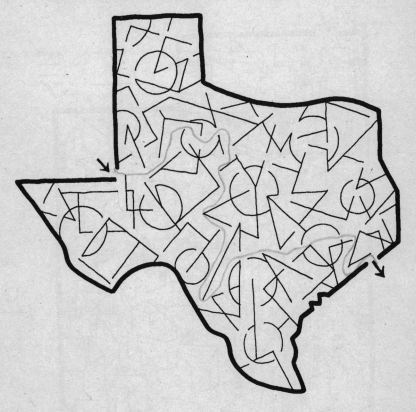

# UTAH

**Capital:** Salt Lake City
**Nickname:** Beehive State
**State Bird:** sea gull
**State Flower:** sego lily

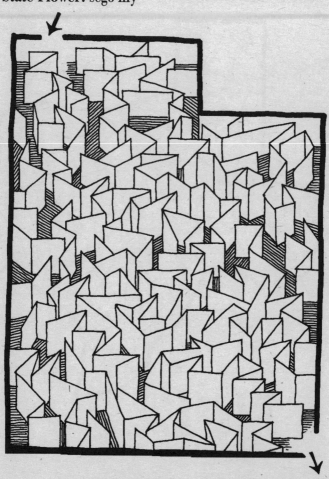

# VERMONT

**Capital:** Montpelier
**Nickname:** Green Mountain State
**State Bird:** hermit thrush
**State Flower:** red clover

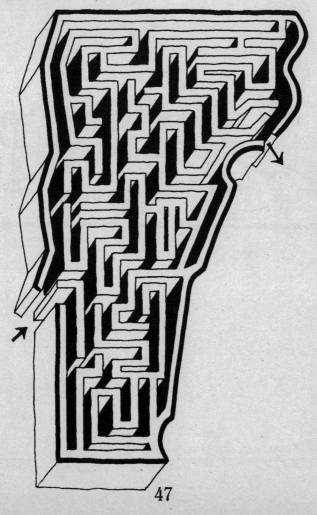

# VIRGINIA

**Capital:** Richmond
**Nickname:** Old Dominion
**State Bird:** cardinal
**State Flower:** dogwood

# WASHINGTON

*Done*

**Capital:** Olympia
**Nickname:** Evergreen State
**State Bird:** willow goldfinch
**State Flower:** coast rhododendron

# WEST VIRGINIA

**Capital:** Charleston
**Nickname:** Mountain State
**State Bird:** cardinal
**State Flower:** rhododendron

# WISCONSIN

**Capital:** Madison
**Nickname:** Badger State
**State Bird:** robin
**State Flower:** wood violet

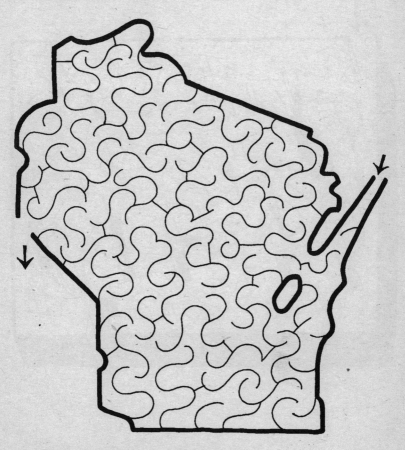

# WYOMING

**Capital:** Cheyenne
**Nickname:** Equality State
**State Bird:** meadowlark
**State Flower:** Indian paintbrush

# Answers

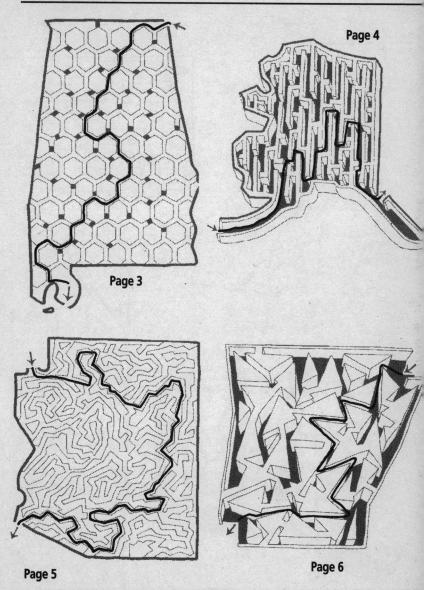

Page 4

Page 3

Page 5

Page 6

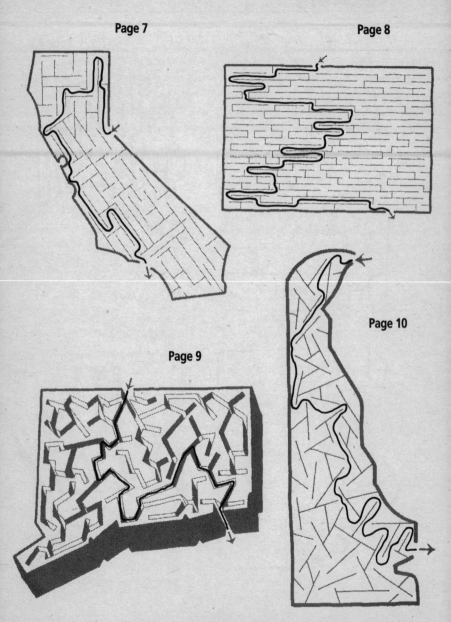

Page 7

Page 8

Page 9

Page 10

54

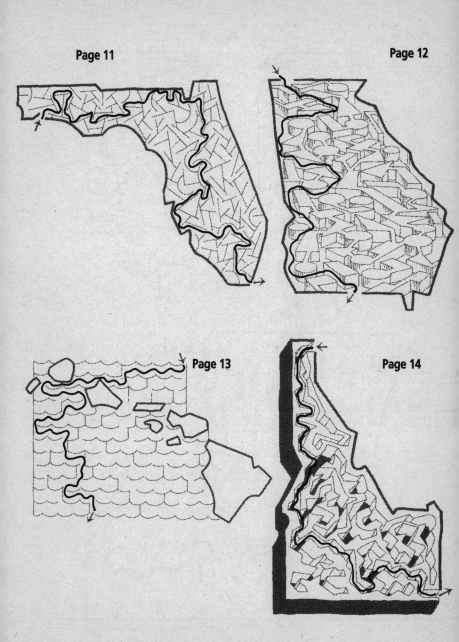

**Page 11**

**Page 12**

**Page 13**

**Page 14**

55

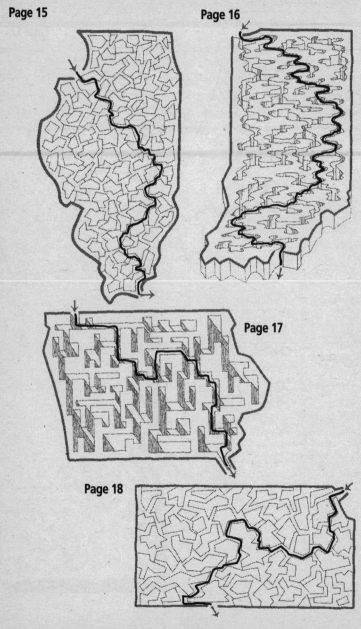

Page 15

Page 16

Page 17

Page 18

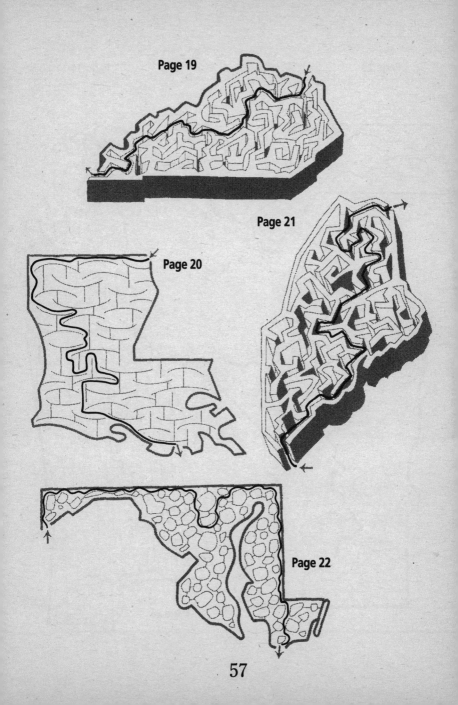

Page 19

Page 21

Page 20

Page 22

57

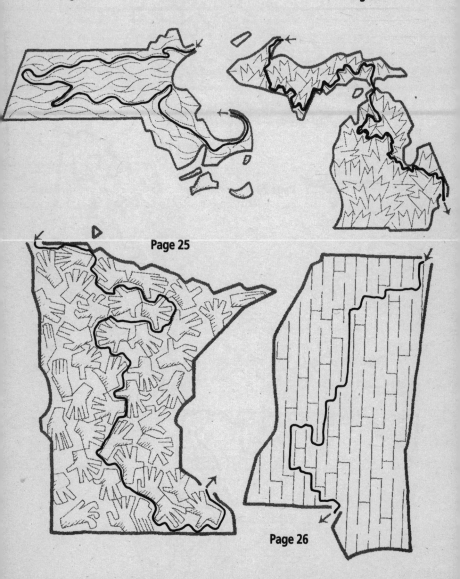

Page 23

Page 24

Page 25

Page 26

58

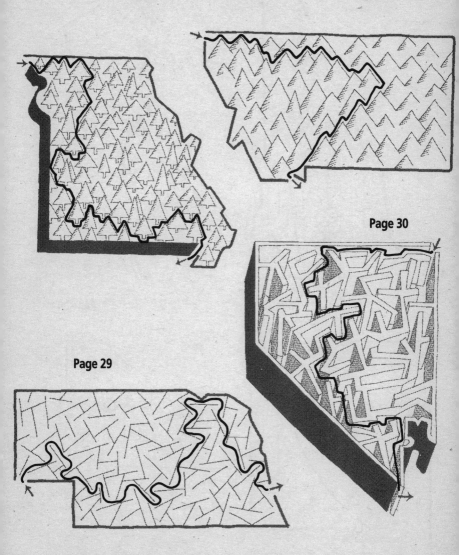

Page 27

Page 28

Page 30

Page 29

59

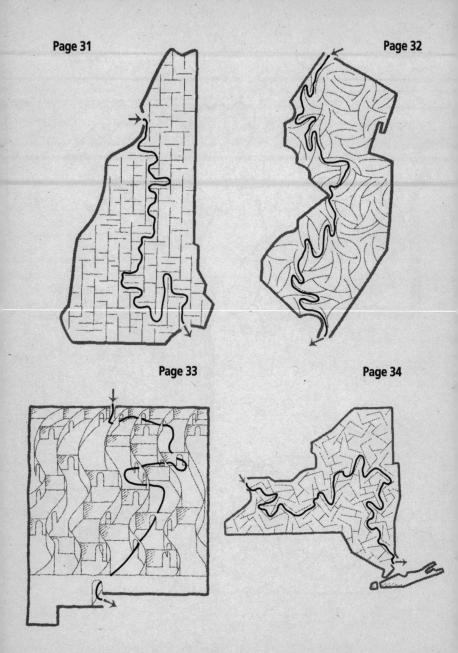

Page 31

Page 32

Page 33

Page 34

60

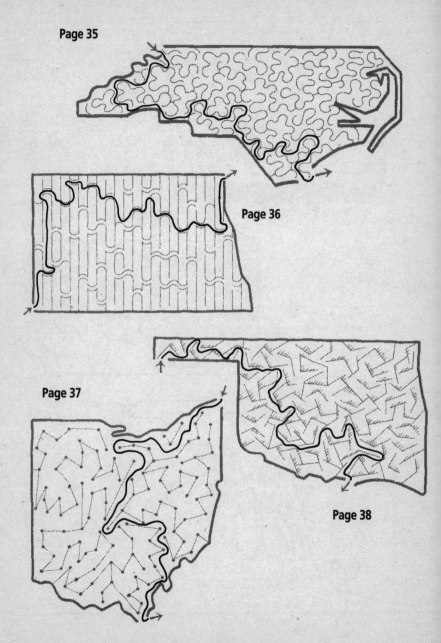

Page 35

Page 36

Page 37

Page 38

61

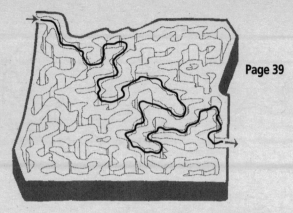

Page 39

Page 40

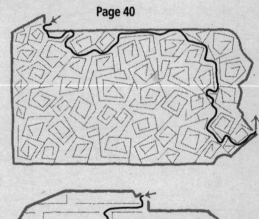

Page 41

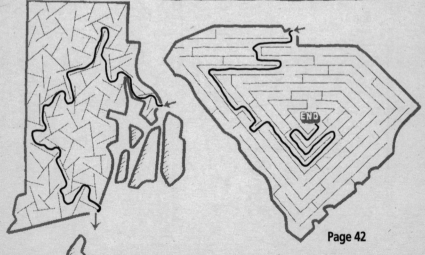

Page 42

62

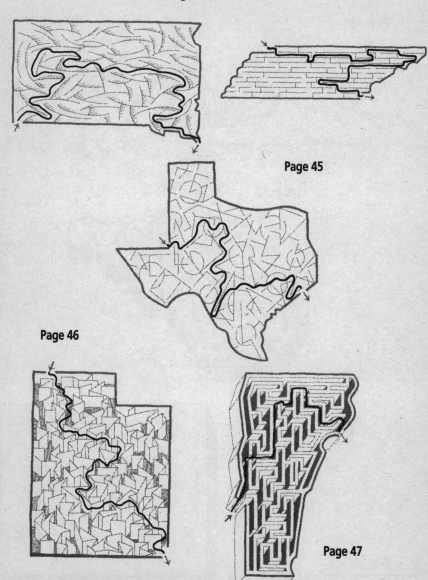

**Page 43**

**Page 44**

**Page 45**

**Page 46**

**Page 47**

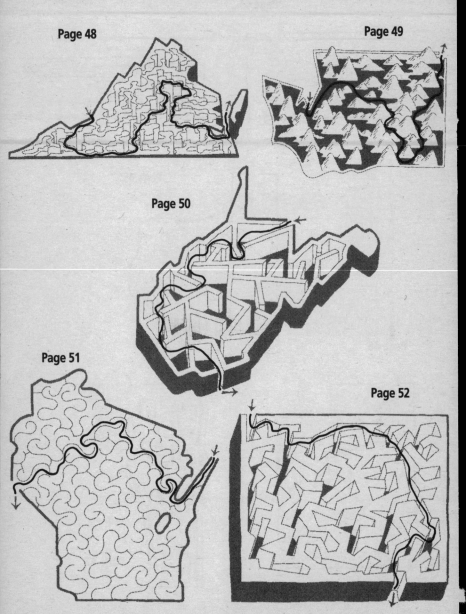

Page 48

Page 49

Page 50

Page 51

Page 52

64